POEMS, PRAYERS, & BLESSINGS

From the Hearts of Chaplains

ARTPACKS

Contributors
Sister Joan Bartosh, Reverend Kitty Burbo, Father James F. Buryska, Father David Byrne, Father Joseph Perumpuzha Chacko, Reverend Alice Durst, Reverend John L. Evans II, Chaplain Mary Feeley, Reverend Priscilla H. Howick, Reverend Daniel R. Johnson, Chaplain Mary E. Johnson, Reverend H. Graciela Jortack, Reverend Dean V. Marek, Reverend Floyd O'Bryan, Father Charles Padathuruthy, Reverend Randall Phillips, Chaplain Katherine M. Piderman, Reverend Ermanno A. Willis

Printed in the United States of America

Published by Artpacks
Rochester, Minnesota, USA
507-273-2529
storymatters@charter.net

Library of Congress Cataloging-in-Publication Data

Poems, prayers, blessings : from the hearts of chaplains.
        p. cm.
    Summary: "A collection of poems, prayers, and blessings
by eighteen hospital chaplains"
    ISBN 978-0-9834637-0-2 (pbk. : alk. paper)
    1. Christian poetry, American. 2. American poetry--21st century.
    PS595.C47P59 2011
    811'.60809212594--dc23
                                2011018591

Cover photograph by *Joseph P. Chacko,*
Typography and design by Virginia Woodruff
The text is set in Nofret Pro

Introduction

Hope is slippery.

Some days it wears hiking boots and assures us that all
will be well and life is our friend.

Other days, Hope hides its face
with barely a shadow offering light.

And then when least expected, Hope jumps out and
grabs us by the heart: You hear another's story of long
days and longer nights, yet you notice a strength in his
voice. Out on the street an image catches your eye and
suddenly you are aware of the Holy right next to you.
Why have I not seen that before?

Poems, Prayers, and Blessings is offered as a gift of Hope
from the hearts of chaplains to all who search. Each
word of blessing, each prayer, each photo is an invitation
to continue listening and welcoming your own story
of Hope.

Hope has a strong heart. It can survive through the
"in between" times of an illness, a loss, dreams that
have to be put on hold, and plans that are suddenly
turned upside down. In exchange, Hope asks for
attention; it needs to be nurtured and pondered and
shared. Our wish is that this small collection might
be a companion for you as you put on your hiking
boots each day and turn another corner in your search.

—Mary Feeley

Contents

Joseph P. Chacko

DISCOVERY

It is incredible when I discover:
That God is present;
That God loves me;
That God knows and understands.

There is power when I discover:
There are things that bind me;
I can be set free;
There is a way through.

I hear a message from Jesus:
I love you;
I am here with you and for you;
I will give you abundant life and peace;
Take my hand, walk with me.

SILENCE

Bleak and barren,
Harbinger of hope,
Dreaded foe,
Blessed guest,
I have known them both.
What makes them different?
The silence or me?

2   *David Byrne*

Suspended Moment

A suspended moment,
measured in time,
yet incomprehensible
that it could be contained
totally within time.

A suspended moment,
reaching deeply down and within
to one's sacred space,
yet always overflowing
freely moving
in an unrehearsed dance.

A suspended moment
embracing a walk
into the human experience,
yet simultaneously evoking a walk
into the Mystery of God
already in embrace.

A suspended moment,
resonating with essence,
truly wordless knowing,
yet stirring the very cell of being
to incredible desire
and profound longing.

A suspended moment!
An incredible embrace
of a beloved God!

Joan Bartosh

Prayer of Blessing for Fetal Remains

God of all creation,
we lift up to You the
mortal remains of this little soul
and ask that You lovingly
receive its spirit
into your embrace.

Please bless this
dream child whose
short journey through life
was too brief for those
who waited in anticipation
of this child's birth.

We ask that, where we
do not understand,
You might sustain us
with Your unending love
weeping with us
over this loss.

In the name of the Father,
and the Son, and the Holy Spirit,
Amen.

Mary E. Johnson

FAREWELL

In memory of Pastor Youa Kao Vang

Good bye, my friend
It's time to go
For you to enjoy
A better life.

Good bye, we say
To you today
May God receive you
In His care.

Your life has been
Not an easy one
May you rejoice
In Jesus Christ.

Our grieving hearts
Tell you "good bye"
Our faithful souls
Sing songs with you.

Good bye dear friend
We say today,
Always alive
You'll be in our hearts.

A PLACE LIKE ANY OTHER

"Where are you from?" I asked, making small talk
with this man—forty years old, maybe less—
as we waited for his daughter to arrive.
"Chicago," in English fluent enough,
though accented. "We came to U.S.A.
from Poland seven years ago." I placed
the accent then. (My ancestors came from
a village near the Polish border.) "Where
in Poland?" I pursued the question. "Oswiecim."
His eyes held questions of their own, alert
if I would recognize the name. Not all
would, but most would identify easily
the German version of the name: Auschwitz.

Visions of electrified, barbed wire
flashed in my head, barracks, chimneys belching
their dreadful smoke. I couldn't help myself.
"What is it like," I blurted, "to live where
there are so many ghosts?" He paused, not sure
he fully understood the question. Then,
"About the same as living anywhere."

I don't know what answer I expected,
but his took me aback at first. Again,
on second thought, why should it? Someone has
to live there. Unless, that is, we don't want
anyone to live there ever again.
Or else demand that those who do, be weighed
by crimes committed before they were born.
A third alternative; forget, or worse,
deny. Instead, we do the best we can:

James Buryska

we build or leave memorials to our
atrocities, our aspirations,
and our victories, and learn to live with them,
alongside them, hoping in time and grace
to sort out which is which. A place
like any other—Oswiecim.

THE TEAR

Please say a prayer for her they said
Her faith means so much to her
I looked over at you in the bed
Your eyes were closed
You were unresponsive
head turned to the side
There was no sign that you could hear us
But your family and I
made a circle around you
Holding hands we prayed
Love and hope
You spoke to us
With the tear
In the corner of your eye

8

LITTLE FLOWER

Little Flower
Bounded by boulders
Seeking the sun/Son
Gracing the gaps
Flourishing

LAUGHING CAT

If you're lucky enough to have
A cat friend
You know the tap, tap of
Her paw on your elbow, your ear,
Your cheek.
LuLu my laughing cat
Taps and slides under my arm.
While I tell her what a
Good cat she is
She licks the icing from my cupcake,
Jumps down
Smiling
To wash her face.

Nature as Soul Comfort Food

In your mind's eye, stroll through a dense woods
and come upon a dancing lake. Delight in the
wisdom of "Friends of Nature" who appear
and companion your mind's eye journey.
Experience the promise, the solitude that heals in:

The subtle QUIET OF THE WOODS that allows
one to drift from the memory of the past days,
no matter what has filled those days.

The gentle sway of SPINDLY TREE TOPS that invites one
into their rhythm and becomes nature's rocking chair.

The dark TREE TRUNKS AND BRANCHES that
hold on to multiple shades of green, sun-illumined
leaves, while here and there a golden matured leaf
comes dancing to the ground.

The movement of SUN-GLISTENING WATER on
a cool lake that mesmerizes one's
attentive soul with its own marvelous "electric show"
of a hundred million flickering white lights.

The crisp, clear AIR that supports life within a
pattern of slow, intentional, deep breathing.

"Friends of Nature," you gift one's soul with the comfort
food of desire that integrates life's happenings while
companioning one to know it is safe to always go deeper!

Joan Bartosh

TOGETHER – WE ARE CHANGED

They come
Some in pain
Some not knowing they are broken within
Some brought by the law
Some walked in by daughters, sons, or lovers.

They come
Because of need
Not because they are eager for change.

At some point, they go
Changed…
Changed…
Wearing bags, braces, casts, canes, patches
Conscious of radiation burns
and chemical companions.

Changed…
Conscious of the burdens of life—
Aware that burdens gave birth to blessings.

They
Our patients
Go.
Changed…
Never the same
Because nothing and no one ever is.

Changed...
Often for better
Sometimes not.

Changed...
Because they seek healing
Because they want to be better.

Changed...
We are
Because of them and us together.

Changed...
We are
Coming here every day
To this holy axis of caring and community
Where nothing stays the same
Except a Presence beyond our imagining.

We come knowing nothing will be the same for
Them and
For us.

Nothing!
Nothing! No thing stays the same!
No body stays the same!

Kitty Burbo

FORGIVENESS

"Father forgive them, for they know not what they do."
—Luke 23: 34 RSV

Jesus, Your words, "Father, forgive them," still echo loudly
in our ears today. The gift of forgiveness:
so yearned for by all,
sometimes so hard to ask for,
sometimes so hard to receive,
sometimes so hard to give.

Yet, as One who must have understood that without
forgiveness, there is no future community of benevolent
and life-giving love.

Yet, as One who must have understood that receiving
or giving the gift of forgiveness would provide
immeasurable peace and joy.

So as You willingly begin your journey of hurt
and injustice, with a heart of love by expressing,
"Father, forgive," so may my life's
journey of hurt and injustice include:
God, forgive them,
Forgive me,
I forgive.

14

Joseph P. Chacko

Emmanuel! God with Us

"We have a worship service on the Rehabilitation Unit tonight.
Would you like to come?" asked the chaplain.
I'll be there!" said the patient. "God's always here for me.
I figure it's up to me to show up
when there is an opportunity to give praise and thanks."
Later, the man "drives" himself to the service
with a device on his wheelchair
that he operates with his mouth.
Emmanuel! Thank you for the signs of Faith among us.

"We've been here for two months,"
said the mother of a patient.
"My daughter's been very sick. She has MS.
It's come on quickly and is very serious."
"How has it been for you?" asked the chaplain.
"Well, it's been so hard. It's like the winter outside—
harsh and dark and very frightening.
But we have the Lord with us.
When I feel the winter overtaking me, I reach deep,
deep down in my soul, and I find spring, a spring
of God's beautiful, comforting promises."
Emmanuel! Thank you for the signs of Hope among us.

Two men were seated beside each other in wheel chairs.
When the time came for the Lord's Prayer,
one man, paralyzed on his left side,
with slow, meticulous determination,
lifted his left arm with his right hand.
He placed his left hand on the right hand
of the man beside him who had quadriplegia.
Emmanuel! Thank you for the signs of Love among us.

Katherine M. Piderman   15

Ritual of Closure for Embryos

God of all creation, on this day at this moment in time
we come before You in humility and in love
to commend to You the spirit
of the life potential held in these embryos.

It is with a sense of awe and reverence that we seek
Your love and presence in this moment. And it is in faith
that we ask Your blessing on this final chapter so that we
may know it is finished, that the life potential is now
at rest, and that we continue with life having been
profoundly changed by this experience.

I pray for this family. Throughout the hopes
and despairs of this experience You have been
with them. As they have anguished over complex
and difficult decisions You have been with them.
As they have attempted to reach a place
of peace You have been with them. May they
continue to feel Your gentle presence guiding them,
holding them, loving them.

We commend the embryos to You now in the name
of the Father, the Son, and the Holy Spirit. Amen.

A Patient's Prayer
to the Eternal Physician

Lord, You are our Eternal Physician
who knows more than anyone in the world
what I need for healing, peace, and comfort!

I pray; doctors treat me for illness; and you bestow on me
healing! Thank you Lord, for loving me into life!

Your healing Spirit renews me—my mind, body, and soul;
strengthen me to face my pain and suffering,
my anxiety and fear!

You enlighten my imagination and thoughts;
help me to discern your designs
and to count your blessings with gratitude!

May my doctors and their teams always have
the necessary words, wisdom, and skills to do
the right thing in right time for me!

May your healing presence
be a balm of solace, comfort, and hope
to those who struggle with pain, suffering, and distress!

Grant that all patients,
especially children, elders, and the lonely,
experience today your healing touch and lasting peace!

Lord, you are our Eternal Physician, who loves me into life;
Heals me and all creation now and always! Amen.

AN INVESTMENT
for Cole

The photo sits on my desk—a snapshot
taken on a cool, summer day, of
an oldster and youngster
walking away from the camera.

We're a matching set, we two:
Big red shirt, small red vest.
scruffy jeans, well worn shoes,
each carrying his tote full of tools.
Hand in hand, we are on our way
to some important job I don't remember.
In the back yard: a fence to fix,
a swing to hang,
a fort to build.

"Cole helping Boppa!" he points to the picture now,
proudly remembering
in his not-quite-three-year-old-way,
how essential it was to the project
that he was the apprentice, the helper.

Happily, he doesn't realize
the job, whatever it was, took twice as long
with his help as without. Never mind.
I didn't need his help that day, but someday,
when we're both older, I will. May it be there—
if not for me, for someone.

James Buryska

Hymn for Carmen and Dominik

Clap your hands! Shout for joy!
Jump as high as you can!
For our wonderful God is always right here!
Close beside us in God's great Spirit way!
Here to guide us whatever we do!
Here to help us to see our way through!

Turn a cartwheel! Reach for the sky!
Sing your favorite song!
For our generous God gives presents of love!
Some we can see and some placed in our hearts!
Gifts that come and never stop!
Love that fills us right up to the top!

Zoom with zip! Cheer with delight!
Use all your crayons to celebrate!
For our powerful God gives us life today!
Our breath and our heartbeats, and even our blood!
Our smiles and our tears, and our wiggles, too!
God gives us all we are and do!

Open your arms...wider...wider...wider!
And give your best and biggest hug to our
wonderful,
generous,
powerful
God!

Bent Shoulders

Your little one walked today
You leaned in front of her
With encouragement
as your heart
filled with tears
Her heart was there too
behind the new incision
laced together with compassion
"Come on you can do it"
"No! It hurts! Please stop!"
And then defiant little feet
Slapped the floor
To the last counts 8...9...10
Staff gave an ovation
While your shoulders curved
from the weight of a parent's love
How bent are God's shoulders

MEMOIR OF HELPING HANDS

I choose to help, not hinder
With my hands so tender;
Pushing, pulling, and always moving,
Ensuring that this one is improving.

I choose to help, not hinder
With these hands I remember;
That this tool inspires transformation,
And gives families consolation.

I choose to help, not hinder
With my hands I render;
A touch that shows I care,
With plenty of love to share.

Joseph P. Chacko

Wisdom of the Way

Having the wisdom to be grateful
is itself a gift from God.
It enables us to walk unafraid
into an unknown future
in the sure knowledge that:

We are bathed in God's love.

God goes before us
and at the same time walks with us.

It is the Way itself that is to be treasured.

Benediction

May the Lord bless and keep you
...in the times of sorrows, trials, and temptations.
May the Lord make His face to shine upon you
...in the darkness of the night.
May the Lord be gracious unto you
...when you feel you have failed.
May the Lord's divine presence be revealed
...during times of doubt and questions.
May the Peace of the Lord
that surpasses human understanding
...be yours today and forever.

AMEN.

PERSPECTIVE

When I
look
at the
bad things
happening
in the world,
And see
all the suffering, pain, from nature, and worse—from fellow
humans, I wonder Why? Why all this heartache? Why do good
people, innocent people suffer? Especially those too young, weak,
ending up drawing a short straw. I find myself asking:
Where
is God
when
this is
happening?
Why doesn't
God do
something
soon?
Now?!
I'm not
alone in my
wondering.
Psalm 13,
How Long
O Lord?
Will you
forget me
forever?
Sometimes
I wonder,
does God
even
know? Care?
Will God
ever do
something
about it?

Randy Phillips

OAKWOOD

It was a proper burial.
Infant, first-born son
processed to the grave
in his father's arms;
tiny casket gently laid on the open earth.

The wailing left no question
about grief's raw-ness, '
the stabbing pain of loss
making breathing difficult
for those who came to stand in solidarity—
young parents, themselves, afraid to move
for fear the Banshee would flay them too.

Someone had placed a tiny bell
in the tree above the grave.
A still morning
graced by an occasional breeze
that urged the bell to ring
at all the right times
so the little spirit
could fly away.

John L. Evans II

A Prayer

Lord, I am a chaplain

It is a work of my heart.
I have been probed and challenged and stretched
and still somehow the faith remains.
Faith that every time I enter a room,
Every time I speak in Your name,
Every time I express compassion,
I do not do so alone.

I am surrounded by a host of angels
Covered by grace and
Guided by the God of creation and love.

They wait for us
Those who are hurting and lost,
Those who long for someone to hold their hand,
Those who recognize Your presence.

How can I not go Lord,
I am a chaplain.

Amen.

WAITING

Three women
waited
for the same

liver

I waited
with them
moving
from room
to room
waiting
with them
for
the same

liver

Sapphire
wanted
It

Opal
wanted
It

Mother of Pearl
hoped for
It

I prayed what
prayer
they desired
Sapphire asked
that no cancer
get in the way
of this liver
need

Opal paced
praying only her
body was
the right
one for the
liver

Mother of Pearl
told me of her
odds
I want it
but I will not hate
anyone if I
do not get the
liver
That picture
on the wall
helps me know
I am
loved

It was Jesus

With equal
angst and
prayer
I waited
with all of them
Sapphire   Opal   Mother of Pearl

At ten o'clock
not knowing
who would get the
liver
I walked from my
office
with a picture
of Jesus
under my
arm

In case
Mother of Pearl
didn't get the
liver
I hoped Jesus
would help her
grieve and go
home
with hope

The Hem of Dying

Does one recognize the
Outlines of dying if
No one tells you its shape or face?

How many mornings did I wake
Hair and face wet with the sweat of fever?
My night's shirt dripping and
Offering reminders of life:
Hunger Cleanup 2001; Sojourner House of Peace:
Drier's Quality Butter; and
Everyone's favorite—ten bright colored heads—
Choose your face for the day.
No one connected those colored faces for me.
Or spoke aloud of dying.

So one hot mid-July afternoon,
I sat with six friends in a tight circle and a
Small bottle of doubly blessed water.
We blessed our lives;
Splashed water on my life:
Gratitude and hope and the hunt for strength.
Julian of Norwich came with "All will be well."
I had never died before but this seemed right.
Weeks later I looked in the mirror and my doc
Looked me straight in the face:
"You touched the hem of dying, and she
Stole your hair."
What I know is that she left me an outline of her face.
What a trick!
But no joke, I continue to splash my
Life with doubly blessed water.

HOPE

Have you ever stopped
to feel the south winds blow?
They are very different
from the cold and cutting north winds.
The south winds are almost warm.
They even smell like warm weather.
They give me the hope of spring
and the promise of summer.
And after a long, cold winter
just the realization of that hope
makes me think about taking off my jacket
and putting on shorts.

Dan Johnson

John L. Evans II

"Blessing" from a Patient

I want you to know
that you inspire me
You use all your skills
and all your creativity
to help me
You serve me
and watch over me
You are God's angel to me
And even when I can not respond
to let you know
that what you do matters
you continue to give me your best
And if God and I find that
my time here is finished
you stay with me
and my loved ones
as long as you are able
Bless your hands
Bless your voice
Bless your skill and training
Bless your heart
And when you are tired
when you are angry because life is unfair
don't ever think that what you do
goes unnoticed
YOU INSPIRE ME

ON THE JOURNEY

When in my wandering
I came upon a dark, deserted house
with nothing to offer but more wandering.
I almost despaired
but there was light
breaking through a boarded window.

A CHAPLAIN'S PRAYER

Help me, O Lord, to be a channel of Your love.
To see in others a fellow creature
that today may need a word or a touch
that reminds them of Your presence.
Help me to care for others compassionately
To hear their deeper needs
To acknowledge their divine nature
To be present to whatever need may present.

Dean V. Marek, Priscilla H. Howick

CONTRIBUTING CHAPLAINS
AT MAYO CLINIC ROCHESTER, MINNESOTA;
JACKSONVILLE, FLORIDA; AND SCOTTSDALE, ARIZONA

Sister Joan Bartosh, SSND, B.A., MPS, BCC, Roman Catholic,
Chaplain in the Neonatal ICU and Respiratory Care Unit, Rochester.

Reverend Kitty Burbo, B.A., M.S., M.Div., United Church of Christ,
Chaplain in the areas of Oncology and Adolescent Psychiatry, Rochester.

Father James F. Buryska, S.T.L., Catholic, Rochester.

Father David Byrne, B.A., Roman Catholic, Rochester.

Father Joseph Perumpuzha Chacko, M.A., BCC, Catholic, Rochester.

Reverend Alice Durst, B.A., M.Div., BCC, ELCA Lutheran,
Chaplain in Cardiac Surgery, Rochester.

Reverend John L. Evans II, B.S., BCC, Catholic, Rochester.

Chaplain Mary Feeley, D.Min, BCC, Rochester.

Reverend Priscilla H. Howick, M.Div., BCC, Director of Chaplain Services, Jacksonville

Reverend Daniel R. Johnson, B.S., Assemblies of God, Hospice Chaplain, Rochester.

Chaplain Mary E. Johnson, M.A., Roman Catholic, Emeritus Chaplain, Rochester.

Reverend H. Graciela Jortack, M.Div., BCC, ELCA Lutheran,
Chaplain in AM Admits and a post-surgical unit and ministers
to Spanish speaking patients, Rochester.

Reverend Dean V. Marek, B.A., BCC, Catholic, retired Chaplain, Rochester.

Reverend Floyd O'Bryan, M.S., BCC, Assemblies of God,
Director of Chaplain Services, Rochester.

Father Charles Padathuruthy, B.Ph., Th.D, BCC, Catholic, Chaplain in Heart and Lung
Transplant, Hematology/Oncology and a Living Donor Advocate, Jacksonville.

Reverend Randall Phillips, M.A., M.Div., BCC, United Methodist, Rochester.

Chaplain Katherine M. Piderman, PhD., BCC, Rochester.

Reverend Ermanno A. Willis, M.Div., BCC, Christian Methodist Episcopal,
Chaplain working in ICU and a Living Donor Advocate, Scottsdale.